National Parks

Glacier

JOANNE MATTERN

Children's Press®
An Imprint of Scholastic Inc.

Content Consultant
James Gramann, PhD
Professor, Department of Recreation, Park and Tourism Sciences
Texas A&M University, College Station, Texas

Library of Congress Cataloging-in-Publication Data
Names: Mattern, Joanne, 1963– author.
Title: Glacier / by Joanne Mattern.
Description: New York, NY : Children's Press, an imprint of Scholastic Inc., [2018] | Series: A true
    book | Includes bibliographical references and index.
Identifiers: LCCN 2017025793 | ISBN 9780531235065 (library binding) | ISBN 9780531238097 (pbk.)
Subjects: LCSH: Glacier National Park (Mont.)—Juvenile literature. | Natural history—Montana—
    Glacier National Park—Juvenile literature.
Classification: LCC F737.G5 M378 2018 | DDC 978.6/52—dc23
LC record available at https://lccn.loc.gov/2017025793

All rights reserved. Published in 2018 by Children's Press, an imprint of Scholastic Inc.
Printed in Heshan, China 62

SCHOLASTIC, CHILDREN'S PRESS, A TRUE BOOK™, and associated logos are trademarks and/or
registered trademarks of Scholastic Inc.

Scholastic Inc., 557 Broadway, New York, NY 10012

1 2 3 4 5 6 7 8 9 10 R 27 26 25 24 23 22 21 20 19 18

Front cover (main): A meadow of wildflowers
Front cover (inset): A kayaker
on Bowman Lake
Back cover: Red Jammer bus on
Going-to-the-Sun Road

Find the Truth!

Everything you are about to read is true *except* for one of the sentences on this page.

Which one is **TRUE**?

T or F   Fur trappers were the first people to see Glacier National Park.

T or F   The ice of the park's glaciers can be up to 100 feet (30.5 m) thick.

Find the answers in this book.

Contents

THE **BIG** TRUTH!

National Parks Field Guide: Glacier

Loon with baby

4

Aspens

Grizzly bear

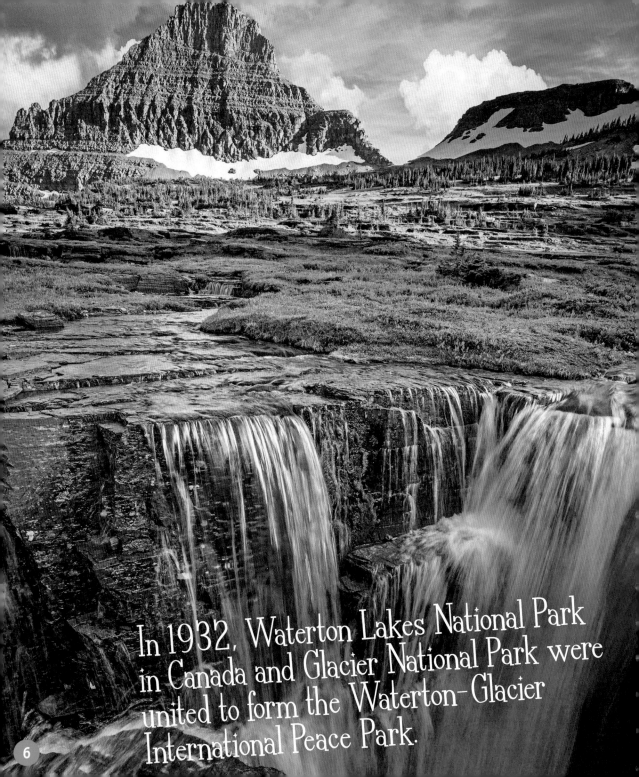

In 1932, Waterton Lakes National Park in Canada and Glacier National Park were united to form the Waterton-Glacier International Peace Park.

CHAPTER 1

A Park Formed by Glaciers

Can you imagine a place where huge, icy **glaciers** streak the sides of towering mountain peaks? Can you picture beautiful green forests growing along the shores of huge, blue lakes? That is exactly what you'll find at Glacier National Park in northwest Montana. Whether you like to hike, camp, or just enjoy the scenery from your car window, you will be amazed at the beauty in the park's natural landscape.

Glacier
National
Park

A Shifting Landscape

About 145 million to
65 million years ago

About 60 million years ago

About 40 million years ago

These maps show how North America changed over millions of years.

Moving Mountains

Billions of years ago, the land that makes up Glacier
National Park was covered by a shallow sea. Over
time, layers of **sediment** sank to the bottom of
the sea. The sediment pressed down to form rock.
Meanwhile, sections of Earth were moving and
shifting. About 70 million to 65 million years ago,
a huge section of rock rose up and slid eastward.
This rock became the mountains that are in Glacier
National Park today.

Shaped by Glaciers

Glacier National Park gets its name from the huge glaciers that shaped its landscape. A glacier forms when snow accumulates faster than it can melt. The weight of the snow on top compresses the lower snow into layers of hardened ice. Pressure from the top layers pushes the bottom layers forward. The glacier moves slowly downhill, cutting into the rocks in its path. Glaciers can carve deep valleys and wear down the sides of mountains. If they melt, they can create deep lakes.

Two separate glaciers carved the tall, thin edge of a rock formation known as the Garden Wall.

The People of Glacier

About 10,000 years ago, people began living in what is now Glacier National Park. By the early 1800s, Native American groups such as the Blackfeet, Salish, and Kootenai called the area home. Around this time, fur trappers began coming to the area from Europe. Later, miners came to dig out the region's copper and gold. As more new settlers arrived, the U.S. government forced Native Americans onto **reservations**.

A Timeline of Glacier National Park

ca. 8000 BCE

Native American people arrive in what is now Montana.

Early 1800s

European explorers and trappers come to the area in search of furs, gold, and other valuable resources.

Glacier Becomes a Park

As more people explored the area, many of them began calling for the region's natural beauty to be preserved. In 1910, President William Howard Taft signed a law to create Glacier National Park. During the early days of the park, most visitors came by train. The Great Northern Railway Company built places for these visitors to stay. Soon, Glacier National Park had become a popular tourist destination.

1892

The Great Northern Railway is built in the area.

1910

President William Howard Taft signs a law to create Glacier National Park.

1932

Going-to-the-Sun Road opens, making it easier for visitors to travel through the park by car.

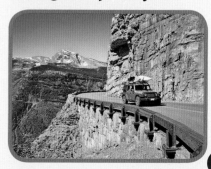

Going-to-the-Sun Road provides visitors easy access to much of Glacier National Park.

Going-to-the-Sun Road

In the early 1900s, it was difficult for visitors to reach some of the park's most beautiful places by car. But in 1921, workers began building a new road that would make the park much more accessible. Eleven years later, in 1932, Going-to-the-Sun Road opened. The road led through the mountains and across the park. The road has been called one of the most beautiful routes in America. It was named a National Historic **Landmark** in 1997.

National Park Fact File

A national park is land that is protected by the federal government. It is a place of importance to the United States because of its beauty, history, or value to scientists. The U.S. Congress creates a national park by passing a law. Here are some key facts about Glacier National Park.

Glacier National Park	
Location	Montana
Year established	1910
Size	1,012,837 acres (409,881 hectares)
Average number of visitors each year	2.9 million
Tallest mountain	Mount Cleveland at 10,466 feet (3,190 meters)
Deepest lake	Lake McDonald at 464 feet (141 m) deep

Bearhat Mountain rises above Hidden Lake in central Glacier National Park.

CHAPTER 2

The Lay of the Land

From the mountaintops to the valleys below, each part of Glacier National Park's landscape holds different wonders. Almost three million people visit every year to experience the park's wide range of natural beauty. They enjoy lakes, waterfalls, and rushing streams. They can explore fields full of flowers or thick mountain forests. They can even climb the park's rocky mountains to get a view from above.

Different types of wildflowers grow at different elevations in the park.

Split Into Three Parts

A section of the Rocky Mountains called the Continental Divide crosses through Glacier National Park. On one side of the divide, water flows west into the Pacific Ocean. On another side, water flows east and ends up in the Gulf of Mexico. In a third section, water flows north into Canada's Hudson Bay. The Continental Divide also splits the park into two different **climates**. The valleys in the western part of the park are warm and wet. East of the mountains, the weather is dry and windy.

The creeks and rivers that flow through Glacier National Park are an important water source for the park's animals.

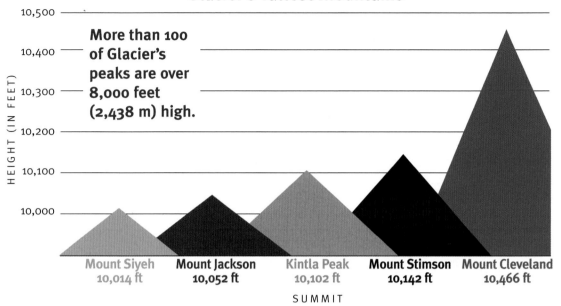

Glacier's Tallest Mountains

More than 100 of Glacier's peaks are over 8,000 feet (2,438 m) high.

HEIGHT (IN FEET)

10,500
10,400
10,300
10,200
10,100
10,000

| Mount Siyeh 10,014 ft | Mount Jackson 10,052 ft | Kintla Peak 10,102 ft | Mount Stimson 10,142 ft | Mount Cleveland 10,466 ft |

SUMMIT

High and Low

Temperatures in the park change depending on **elevation**. Mountain peaks are very cold. Some have snow year-round. Glacier's highest peak is Mount Cleveland, at 10,466 feet (3,190 m) tall. Other tall mountains include Mount Siyeh, Mount Jackson, and Mount Gould. Below the mountains lie numerous valleys. There, temperatures can reach above 90 degrees Fahrenheit (32 degrees Celsius) in summer.

Wonderful Water

There are 762 lakes in Glacier National Park. The largest is Lake McDonald. This lake is almost 10 miles (16 km) across and about 500 feet (152 m) deep. High mountains surround it and reflect off the water's clear surface. Swiftcurrent Lake is a popular destination for visitors, who can hike around the lake or take a boat out on its waters. The lake is full of fish, including trout. Moose also like to drink along the edges of the water.

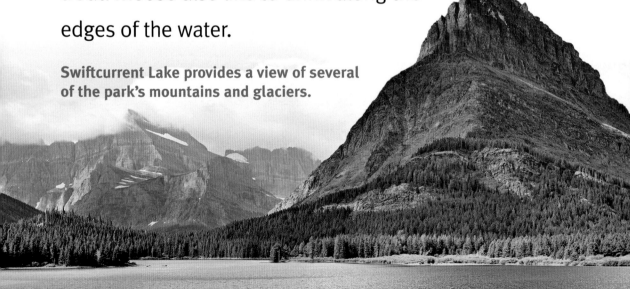

Swiftcurrent Lake provides a view of several of the park's mountains and glaciers.

Throughout Glacier, many streams rush down the sides of mountains. Sometimes they crash over cliffs in beautiful waterfalls. All of this water comes from snow melting in the mountains in the spring. After the snow stops melting, many of the streams dry up. However, some

Virginia Falls is a popular spot for hikers to visit.

keep flowing all year long. One notable waterfall is Virginia Falls, where water drops 50 feet (15 m) straight down before crashing into Virginia Creek.

Land of Glaciers

The main attractions of Glacier National Park are, of course, the glaciers! The largest ones cover as much as 0.6 square mile (2 square kilometers) of land. Some, such as Jackson Glacier, are up to 100 feet (30.5 m) thick! However, the park's glaciers used to be much bigger. Climate change has caused much of their ice to melt over the years.

Jackson Glacier was once part of Blackfoot Glacier. As Blackfoot shrank over time, it separated into two glaciers.

George Bird Grinnell

George Bird Grinnell was the editor of a popular magazine about outdoor activities such as hunting, fishing, camping, and hiking. In 1885 and 1887, Grinnell explored northwestern Montana and became the first European man to see the glacier that now bears his name. Grinnell loved the area so much that he returned there many times. He also helped convince the U.S. government to make the area a national park.

Animals Big and Small

Because Glacier National Park has such a diverse range of **ecosystems**, it is also home to an amazing range of animals. Tiny insects buzz through the air as huge mammals wander among the trees. The water is packed with fish, and birds of all kinds flit through the air.

There are 29 species of birds of prey in Glacier National Park.

Living Large

Black bears are North America's most common bear species.

Bears are some of the largest animals you'll find in the park. Male grizzly bears can weigh more than 450 pounds (204 kilograms) and be up to 6 feet (2 m) tall. Black bears are smaller than grizzlies, but they can still weigh up to 250 pounds (113 kg). These animals can be very dangerous. Visitors to the park are advised to stay at least 100 yards (91.4 m) away from any bears they see.

Large mammals such as elk, deer, and moose are found throughout the park. Moose are the largest animals in the park. They like to live alone. Elk and deer live in large herds. They roam the meadows and graze on grass and other plants. Gray wolves, among the park's fiercest **predators**, hunt the elk, deer, moose, and other animals.

The moose is the largest species in the deer family.

Small Mammals

Smaller mammals such as squirrels, mice, and pikas scurry across the ground, while little brown bats zoom through the night sky. Beavers build dams on the water. Marmots are stocky animals that eat grass and other plants and live in underground burrows. Mountain goats are found up on the park's rocky peaks. These animals have special hooves that help them climb the sides of steep cliffs.

The mountain goat is the official symbol of Glacier National Park.

Feathers in the white-tailed ptarmigan's nostrils help warm the frigid air as it enters the bird's nose.

Birds of a Feather

The park is home to 276 bird species. Some, such as the bald eagle and the golden eagle, are large predators. Bald eagles nest high in the trees. They swoop down to grab fish out of the park's lakes and streams. The white-tailed ptarmigan lives in the **alpine** areas of the park. Its white feathers help it blend in with the snow. This bird also has feathers on its feet to keep them warm in the snow.

Trout can be found in many bodies of water across the park.

Fish and Insects

With so many bodies of water, Glacier National Park provides plenty of homes for fish. The streams are filled with several kinds of trout. There are also whitefish in the lakes.

Insects are an important part of the park's ecosystems. They provide food for many animals and help plants grow. Some of the park's most common insects are ladybugs and butterflies. The glacier stonefly is found only in the cold glacial streams in Glacier National Park.

Reptiles and Amphibians

Because the weather is often very cold in most of the park, few reptiles and amphibians can survive there. **Cold-blooded** animals such as these have a difficult time surviving low temperatures. Glacier's only three reptile species are the Western painted turtle and two kinds of garter snakes. Its six amphibian species include four kinds of frogs, one kind of toad, and one kind of salamander.

Common garter snakes may squirt a bad-smelling fluid if they think they're in danger.

National Parks Field Guide: Glacier

Field guides have helped people identify wildlife and natural objects from birds to rocks for more than 100 years. Guides usually contain details about appearance, common locations, and other basics. Use this field guide to discover six animals you can spot in the park, and learn fascinating facts about each one!

Canadian lynx

Scientific name: *Lynx canadensis*

Habitat: Subalpine forests

Diet: Rabbits, rodents, birds

Fact: These cats are mostly active at night.

Moose

Scientific name: *Alces alces*

Habitat: Forests near lakes and swamps

Diet: Grass and the leaves of water plants

Fact: Moose don't like it when the temperature gets too warm. They stay cool by taking a dip in a lake or stream on a hot day.

Little brown bat

Scientific name: *Myotis lucifugus*

Habitat: Caves and trees

Diet: Insects

Fact: Bats are the only mammals that can fly.

Golden eagle

Scientific name: *Aquila chrysaetos*

Habitat: Mountains and open meadows

Diet: Small mammals, reptiles, birds

Fact: Golden eagles grab their prey with their sharp talons.

Common loon

Scientific name: *Gavia immer*

Habitat: Lakes

Diet: Fish

Fact: Common loons are black and white in the summer, but turn gray and white in the winter.

Western painted turtle

Scientific name: *Chrysemys picta*

Habitat: Ponds, lakes, marshes

Diet: Earthworms, insects, water plants

Fact: During the winter, this turtle hibernates in the mud at the bottoms of lakes or ponds.

The Park's Plants

Glacier National Park is home to an amazing variety of plants growing in different areas. Some plants flourish in the warmer, wetter parts of the park. Others can only grow in the cold mountains. From the cedar and pine forests in the west to the flowers and bushes that grow in the lower elevations, Glacier is packed with plants.

Tall trees provide homes for many mammals, birds, and insects.

East and West

The warmer western part of the park features cedar and hemlock forests. Some of the trees in these forests have been growing for hundreds of years. White spruces and cottonwoods grow at lower elevations. Ferns and moss grow on the damp forest floor.

The eastern part of the park is cooler and drier. The trees here are mostly aspens. Grassy meadows are also a common sight.

High Elevations

Tundra is found in the highest elevations. Here, tiny flowers and lichens grow on the rocks and in the shallow soil. Sturdy evergreens grow at the edge of the **treeline**.

Lichen

Beargrass

Middle Elevations

Spruce and poplar trees grow in the middle elevations. In wetter areas, thick forests of cedar and hemlock are common. Some of these trees are more than 500 years old!

Cedar

Spruce

Low Elevations

At lower elevations, ferns and moss grow on the forest floor, while meadows are filled with grasses and colorful wildflowers. In river valleys, the leaves of aspen trees turn brilliant yellow and orange in the fall.

Ferns

Aspen

The park's worst fire season in history occurred in 2003, when more than 135,000 acres (54,633 ha) of forest burned.

CHAPTER 5

Looking Toward the Future

Like many natural habitats, Glacier National Park faces many different problems. Although the land, plants, and animals are protected by laws, disasters can still harm the park. Some of these disasters are natural, while others are created by humans. For example, Glacier has serious problems with forest fires. Most of these fires are caused by lightning strikes, but some are the result of human carelessness.

Too Many People

Glacier has millions of visitors every year. Some of these people leave litter. If they go off marked trails, they can damage plants and natural features. Cars and buses bring pollution into the park's air.

In recent years, land outside the park has been mined and logged. Many buildings are also being built. These changes can affect the area's natural balance and the animals that move in and out of the park. ★

Glacier National Park is busiest in the summer.

Shepard Glacier, 1913

Shepard Glacier, 2005

Shrinking Glaciers

Perhaps the biggest challenge facing Glacier National Park is climate change. In 1850, the park had 150 glaciers. Today, it has 25. As our planet warms, the glaciers melt away. Scientists predict all the park's glaciers will be gone by 2030. Shrinking glaciers means less and warmer water in the streams. This can harm the fish there. Climate change may also affect where plants can grow, which in turn affects the animals that eat them.

Scientists do not think we can stop the effects of climate change in the park. What we can do is study its effects and educate visitors.

Map Mystery

One of the most popular places to stay in the park is near a famous lake. Follow the directions below to find the answer.

Directions

1. Start at the Visitor Center at the eastern edge of the park.

2. Sail southwest along the lake that shares its name with the Visitor Center where you began.

3. Climb over the mountains through the pass, or gap, west of the lake.

4. Head southwest toward the road that was named a National Historic Landmark in 1997.

5. When you reach a large lake, you'll see the lodge where people love to stay.

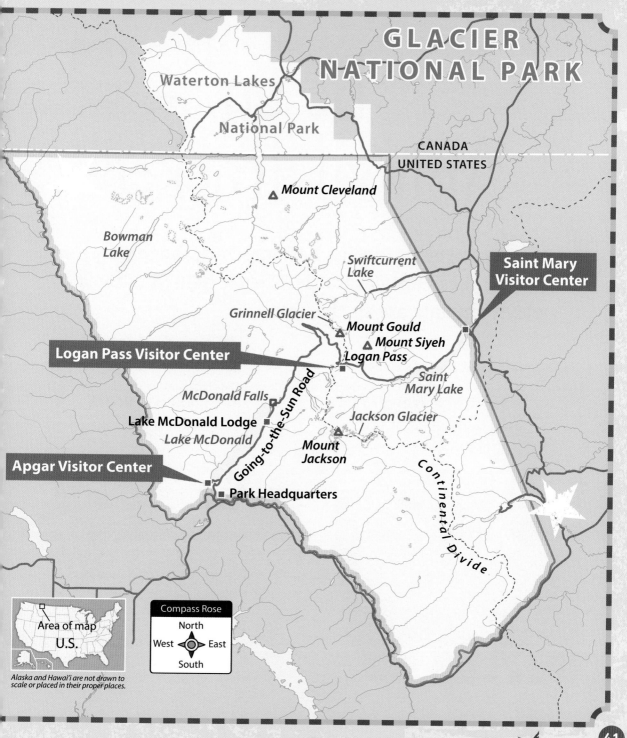

GLACIER NATIONAL PARK

Waterton Lakes

National Park

CANADA
UNITED STATES

△ Mount Cleveland

Bowman
Lake

Swiftcurrent
Lake

Grinnell Glacier

**Saint Mary
Visitor Center**

△ Mount Gould

△ Mount Siyeh

Logan Pass Visitor Center

Logan Pass

Saint
Mary Lake

McDonald Falls

Jackson Glacier

Lake McDonald Lodge

Going-to-the-Sun Road

Lake McDonald

Mount
Jackson

△

Apgar Visitor Center

Continental Divide

■ **Park Headquarters**

Compass Rose

North

West ◆ East

South

Area of map
U.S.

*Alaska and Hawai'i are not drawn to
scale or placed in their proper places.*

Be an Animal Tracker!

If you're ever in Glacier National Park, keep an eye out for these animal tracks. They'll help you know which animals are in the area.

Grizzly bear

Paw length: 9 to 12 inches (23 to 30.5 centimeters)

Gray wolf

Paw length: 4.5 inches (11.5 cm)

Marmot
Paw length: 3.5 inches (9 cm)

Mountain goat
Hoof length: 3.5 inches (9 cm)

Elk
Hoof length: 5 to 6 inches (12.5 to 15 cm)

Ring-necked pheasant
Foot length: 3 inches (7.5 cm)

True Statistics

Number of glaciers: 25

Number of mountains: 175

Total length of streams inside the park: 2,865 mi. (4,610 km)

Number of waterfalls: 200

Number of lakes: 762

Total length of trails in the park: 746 mi. (1,200 km)

Number of fish species in the park: 24

Number of mammal species: 71

Number of bird species: 276

Did you find the truth?

F Fur trappers were the first people to see Glacier National Park.

T The ice of the park's glaciers can be up to 100 feet (30.5 m) thick.

Resources

Books

Flynn, Sarah Wassner, and Julie Beer. *National Parks Guide U.S.A.* Washington, DC: National Geographic, 2016.

Graf, Mike. *Glacier National Park: Going to the Sun*. Guilford, CT: FalconGuides, 2012.

Stein, R. Conrad. *Montana*. New York: Children's Press, 2015.

Visit this Scholastic website for more information on Glacier National Park:
★ www.factsfornow.scholastic.com
Enter the keyword **Glacier**

Important Words

alpine (AL-pine) having to do with mountains

climates (KLYE-mits) the weather typical of places over a long period of time

cold-blooded (KOHLD BLUHD-id) having a body temperature that changes according to the temperature of the surroundings

ecosystems (EE-koh-sis-tuhmz) all the living things in places and their relation to their environments

elevation (el-uh-VAY-shuhn) height above sea level

glaciers (GLAY-shurz) slow-moving masses of ice found in mountain valleys or polar regions

landmark (LAND-mahrk) a building or place selected and pointed out as important

predators (PREH-duh-turz) animals that hunt other animals for food

reservations (rez-ur-VAY-shuhnz) areas of land set aside by the government for a special purpose

sediment (SED-uh-muhnt) rocks, sand, or dirt carried to a place by water, wind, or ice

treeline (TREE-line) the highest or farthest north point at which trees can grow

tundra (TUHN-druh) a very cold area where there are no trees and the soil under the surface of the ground is always frozen

Index

Page numbers in **bold** indicate illustrations.

About the Author

Joanne Mattern has written more than 250 books for children. She especially likes writing about all the amazing places on our planet. Joanne also loves to write about animals, plants, and the natural world. She grew up in New York State and still lives there with her husband, four children, and several pets.